THE
POET'S HOUSE

An anthology of poems

chosen by
JUDE BRIGLEY

illustrated by
FRAN EVANS

PONT *poetry*

First Impression—2000
Second Impression—2001

ISBN 1 85902 602 8

© text: the poets

© illustrations: Fran Evans

This book is published with the support
of the Arts Council of Wales.

Printed in Wales at
Gomer Press, Llandysul, Ceredigion SA44 4QL

To
G. D. Richards
my best teacher

CONTENTS

IN THE POET'S PLAYROOM

THE POET'S HALL OF HEROES

THE POET'S PITCH

Welcome to the poet's house then,
Which today proudly is on show.
We'll take you through with pleasure
Inform you, with the words you need to know.

For this house is full of wonders
That will make you gasp with awe
Or maybe weep some heart-felt tears,
Make you laugh at what you saw.

The poet's house is full of windows:
Each one offers up a separate view.
Each room suggests a different story
And every single one of them is true.

Titles

INK
to be used
drawing &

Utensils

Letters

commas

full-stops

•The Poet's Kitchen•

I am Taliesin. I sing a perfect metre

I am Taliesin. I sing perfect metre,
Which will last to the end of the world.
My patron is Elphin ...

I know why there is an echo in a hollow;
Why silver gleams; why breath is black; why liver is
bloody;
Why a cow has horns; why a woman is affectionate;
Why milk is white; why holly is green;
Why a kid is bearded; why the cow-parsnip is hollow;
Why brine is salt; why ale is bitter;
Why the linnet is green and berries red;
Why a cuckoo complains; why it sings;
I know where the cuckoos of summer are in winter.
I know what beasts there are at the bottom of the sea;
I know how many spears in battle; how many drops in a
shower;
Why a river drowned Pharaoh's people;
Why fishes have scales,
Why a white swan has black feet ...

I have been a blue salmon,
I have been a dog, a stag, a roebuck on the mountain,
A stock, a spade, an axe in the hand,
A stallion, a bull, a buck,
A grain which grew on a hill,
I was reaped, and placed in an oven,
I fell to the ground when I was being roasted
And a hen swallowed me.
For nine nights was I in her crop.
I have been dead, I have been alive,
I am Taliesin.

Taliesin

The Thin Prison

Hold the pen close to your ear.
Listen—can you hear them?
Words burning as a flame,
Words glittering like a tear,

Locked, all locked in the slim pen.
They are crying for freedom.
And you can release them,
Set them running from prison.

Himalayas, balloons, Captain Cook,
Kites, red brick, London Town,
Sequins, cricket bats, large brown
Boots, lions and lemonade—look,

I've just let them out!
Pick up your pen, and start,
Think of the things you know—then
Let the words dance from your pen.

Leslie Norris

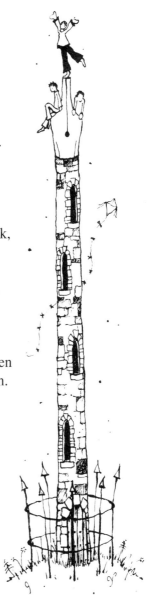

Proverbs and Sayings from the Roadside

It's a long, long trench
that has no turning

Never take five
when you can take six

It takes two
to lift a shovel

Too many foremen
spoil the job

A foreman's work
is never done

Look up
before you light up

Holes have ears

It's an ill pick
that strikes a cable

Rolling stones
knock you silly

Drills should be seen
and not heard

Watch your toes
and your feet will look after themselves

Count your wages
before you get them

A pint in the Bird in Hand
is worth two in the Bush

Muck is cleaner
on the other side

People who live in mansions
should be stoned

Navvys might fly

As you dig your hole
so you must lie in it.

Alan Perry

Words

They are stones
shaped to the hand.
Fling them accurately.

They are horses.
Bridle them;
they'll run away with you.

They are windows,
opening on vistas
that are unreachable.

They are apples.
Bite on hardness
to the sweet core.

They are coracles;
flimsy,
soon overloaded.

They are candles.
Carry them carefully.
They have burned cities.

Catherine Fisher

The Poet's Lounge.

I'm in Love with the Girl at Tesco's Check-out Till

I shall never forget that face
The day I bought a chocolate mousse.
As it melted in my hand
A fairy waved its magic wand
And I fell in love
With the girl
At the Tesco's checkout till.

'That's 15p' she said to me.
Counting my luck
As I counted the coins
Then I slipped my money
Into her fragile hands
And said, 'Thankyou very much'
With all my charm.
With the grace of a swan
She gave me the receipt
The perfect souvenir
For me to keep.
Now every time I eat a chocolate mousse
I think of her.

Sean Dudson

Trying It On

I used to sneak into my sister's room
when she was out.
I pinched her lipstick, made my mirrored mouth
a cherry pout.

One time I found this bronzing tube and creamed
my spotty face.
By break I was a tan-streaked member of
the Asian race.

The Head was mad and wrote a letter home—
my Mam was tamping.
She banned me from the treasure drawers and
left me stamping.

She said, 'No more of that, young brazen miss!'
(like brass, it means).
Instead I tried on heaps of sister-clothes,
her tops and jeans.

When I am sixteen I will be a model,
look so ultra-cool.
It's not fair I can't have stuff of my own
to make boys drool.

I peeked in when our Anne was kissing Dai,
just for some tips.
She caught me, threw a shoe and said,
'You're pushing your luck, you are!'

Jean Gill

My Box

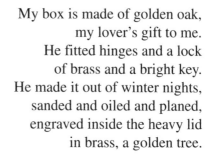

My box is made of golden oak,
my lover's gift to me.
He fitted hinges and a lock
of brass and a bright key.
He made it out of winter nights,
sanded and oiled and planed,
engraved inside the heavy lid
in brass, a golden tree.

In my box are twelve black books
where I have written down
how we have sanded, oiled and planed,
planted a garden, built a wall,
seen jays and goldcrests, rare red kites,
found the wild heartsease, drilled a well,
harvested apples and words and days
and planted a golden tree.

On an open shelf I keep my box.
Its key is in the lock.
I leave it there for you to read,
or them, when we are dead,
how everything is slowly made,
how slowly things made me,
a tree, a lover, words, a box,
books and a golden tree.

Gillian Clarke

Iron Age Girl

The wind weaves her hair
up from her neck.
Here in the hill fort
cross patterns of land
reveal secrets
to a slow sift of sky.
Once she lived this life;
we find her beads,
fragments of pots.

I now walk in her paths
gleaning knowledge of her living,
gathering atmosphere,
piecing her life together.
She'd pluck wool from soay sheep,
spin a fine, strong thread,
dye it in blackberry, or rosehip,
weave her interlacing threads
into a tunic to keep out cold.

I write her history—
she has no name.
I hear her harp;
her voice strong in wind
is a tangle against the gorse.

Sue Moules

The Music Is

I stand between the notes of the scale
Awaiting my release,
To all who miss me—misery,
To all who find me—peace.

The music is
The music was
The music ever will
The music enters into space
And all that follows is still.

The man who takes me for a friend
Will never be alone,
May all who find me celebrate
May all who miss me moan.
May all who miss me curse and cry
May all who miss me fade and die
May all who miss me wonder why
May all who miss me drown.

The oboe keeps me company
The cello soothes my brow
The trumpet wakes me from my sleep
The flute it shows me how to weep ...
To dance, to sing, do anything,
The flute it shows me how.

The music is
The music was
The music ever will
The music empties into space
And all that follows is still.

I know my time, I know my place,
I sing in every key,
But wherever you look you'll find I'm gone
I'm where I used to be

I'm where I am
I'm where I'm not
I was here before you came,
Release me from my silent tomb
And join me in my game.

Phillip Jackson

Thank you Letter

Dear Truelove,
Thank you for the pear tree
and the partridge so auspicious;
the fruit tree's in the garden
and the partridge was delicious.
And thank you for the turtle doves,
French hens and colly birds . . .
(The carpet's at the cleaners) . . .
I can hardly find the words
to say how much I treasure
five rings you sent as well . . .
The geese and swans a-swimming
only added to the smell!
You sent eight maids a-milking,
nine drummers came next day . . .
The eight maids all have boyfriends . . .
(The ninth one didn't stay.)
The pear tree hasn't taken,
leaves have withered on the bough,
the swans attacked the turtle doves,
the geese make such a row . . .
Two French hens are broody,
colly birds have flown the coop . . .
Yes, I realise you sent me three . . .
the third is chicken soup.
Ten pipers stand outside my door
to fill my flowing cup.
My head's already aching
and they're only tuning up!
The eleven ladies dancing
really are the end . . .

The leaping lords are just too much . . .
They drive me round the bend!
So, Merry Christmas truelove,
my faith in you's unbroken,
but next year, please, remember . . .
I'd prefer a C.D. token.

Brian Smith

I love your shoes

I hate your clothes.
You've got no taste.
But I like the way
Your shoes are laced.

I hate your smile.
I hate your face.
But your shoes
They're no disgrace.

You've got no charm.
You act the fool.
But I really think
Your shoes are cool.

I've got something to say
And nothing to lose.
I'd like to tell you
That I love your shoes.

Claire Payne

The Think

Alone, aloud, it wakes once more
Behind the locks of the mind's door.
It feeds on what drink left behind
And now the Think stalks another mind.
Alone, in darkness, the mawling starts
Poisoning icons, opening hearts.

Into clefts the Think will creep
When men dream safe, asleep.
Stirring waters, blood riptides
Amongst the ghosts the Think will hide.
Dark life monsters it will devour
Between the eve and the witching hour.

Between the ears as a sane sole frets
The Think works and sits and sweats.
With caves of doubt and chasms of fear
Spawning young the Think will appear
Stillborn, live, its offspring spread
Marching silently through the head.

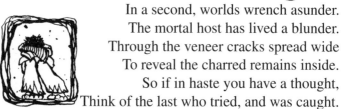

In a second, worlds wrench asunder.
The mortal host has lived a blunder.
Through the veneer cracks spread wide
To reveal the charred remains inside.
So if in haste you have a thought,
Think of the last who tried, and was caught.

Gareth Jones

26

·The Poet's Rucksack·

The Old Wise Teacher introduces her favourite pupil to a book

Press that red button.
The drawer will open.
Take the forbidden fruit.
There is an heirloom
From the twentieth century.
Hold it and you hold back
The hands of time
From this symbol of wisdom.
Its mouth of knowledge
Opens wide, its leaves fluttering.
It links you to past worlds
And as you follow
The footprints
Down its snowy sheets
Take your unused time
With both hands
And be enlightened,
From the icy path
Of technocrats
Who guided you
To oblivious exits.
Learn and know
That this is a book.

Zoe Brigley

Pencils

Six, in a box of Chinese lacquer,
smelling of sandalwood,
each in its roll of marbled paper.

One for a neglected letter;
whims, an arbitrary mood
stroked to that deft, unchanging order.

One for sketching the blown boughs,
quickly, in haste,
fixing the season's throes.

And the poem will claim one, that's sure;
selfish, it will waste
itself, eat itself up with pleasure.

The fourth on a plan of fields will mark
secret places; a gate
in a lane for leaning on, a tree by a lake.

Another will weave a story; reason
and folly in a tight net.
This too will entrap the seasons.

The last is a silent danger.
Let it lie like a wand.
One day I'll open the box and unleash its power.

Catherine Fisher

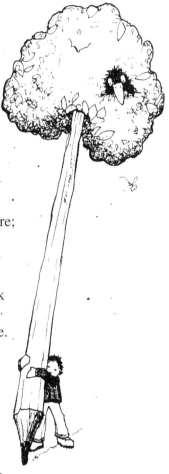

Desk

I rescued you, splinted your broken legs.
Forty years or so had scummed you dark
With ink, dead skin, the rain of dust, the grease
Of knees and cuffs and fingertips, with work

Done routinely by the bored but paid.
I unlidded you, cut wedges, made true
The skewed split joints, machined human gluten
Off the boards. My carpentry of nails and glue

Fell short of craft but was informed by love.
I plugged you, cleaned your handles, planed,
Saw purity of copper and the packed white grain.
Some wounds were healed, the depth of others learned

—No restoration ever is complete.
People at work, the children and the staff,
Gave you their own disfigurement—
Not inborn malice but the hurt of graft

That rubbed a hole in their humanity.
And I played Samaritan out of guilt
Of sorts. Worked out, I was looking for my
Small re-creation as you were rebuilt.

Relidded, drawers eased, your eight legs firm,
Beeswax bringing alive the fans and bars
Of tan and yellow grain, you are a place
For another sort of work. We're both scarred

But the worm in each of us is dead.
I'm not paid much, but neither am I bored
Nor hurt by work's attrition as we go
To real work. This page, the silence, these words.

Christopher Meredith

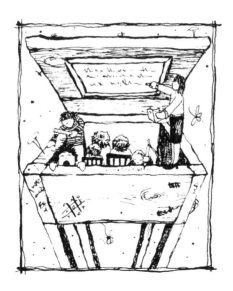

Back to School

It's time you were off, Jonnie. What did we say?
That we're not going to have any upsets today,
that we're going to be brave and we're not going to cry
and it's … What sort of knot d'you call that, in your tie?

Well, it's not what I'd … Oh, you look smart, oh you do,
but how long will it last? Have you been to the loo?
A bit of luck, really, in finding that sweater …
No, stand still a minute, I'll just … there, that's better.

Oh, honestly! You and your buttons. I think …
There we are. No, it's you. They don't make them to
                                                    shrink.
I could take you to school, but I'll not see you in.
Well, for one thing, I'm not sure I'd cope with the din.

And then stuck inside thinking … what? Oh, to be free?
But you've got to be somewhere, so why not 3B?
In the quest to be best, in the good and the bad,
really, all things considered, I'm really quite glad

that I've left that particular battle behind.
But I'll tell you one thing that I've ... no, never mind.
You'll be better off there than outside in the rain ...
and your friends—you've been longing to see them again.

You said once or twice that you wished you were back.
That reminds me, do keep a look out for your mac.
Could you ask? I don't know, but it can't disappear,
and it was meant to last you the rest of the year.

I'll try and look out something special for tea.
Oh, I don't know—something—surprise, wait and see.
Oh, and zip up your coat if it does come on wet,
and have you got a hankie? I knew you'd forget.

Well, there are some upstairs, yes, in one of your drawers.
Goodness knows what you keep in those pockets of yours.
So you'll go on your own. Goodness, just think, September,
the end of the holidays, but I remember ...

when you first ... d'you want anything for the break?
Have you got everything you were going to take?
Your wallet? Your cheque-book, your pipe and your keys?
And don't lose your temper with 3B, love, please.

So I'll come and collect you then, just after three,
and take you home, safe and sound, ready for tea.
It isn't a problem, just more of a knack,
getting teacher to school on the first morning back.

John Bilsborough

Howard

At poison-touch in the schoolyard
You had to hold yourself
Where the poisoner laid his hand.
I was the last to be tracked down,

And Howard fetched me such a ringing clatsh
Across the ear that I watched stars
Swim like the hundreds and thousands
My mother might scatter on a sponge cake.

So clutching a sore temple
I joined the hunt to catch
The only boy in school to bear no mark.
Up the embankment he led the sprint,

Kicking through a drift
Of black-spotted sycamore leaves,
Retreating as we slowly circled round.
After all, this was someone

Who required our arms' length respect.
Wild as a hawk
Was the village verdict
Passed on a jug-eared Lucifer,

An eleven-year-old
With freckles as big as rice grains,
Who would march his enemies
The length of the crumbling school wall

Above a church plantation
Turned to wilderness,
The thorns on the briar-arms
Black as flagon shards.

And as we closed I saw him smile
In a face wrinkling like silver paper,
His coif the colour of new rope
Brushing under our outstretched hands

As he raced into truancy's legends
Of river-dumped books, girls
Knocked up, and bus-station
Prescriptions of benzedrine.

That last time he was glimpsed, a lifetime on,
He wore a Persian-blue
Airforce greatcoat, the Piccadilly
Neon cruel in his face,

Before stepping, our prisoner,
Too swift for the game,
Into a doorway and vanishing,
Still skilled, it seemed, at making an escape.

Robert Minhinnick

I'm not getting up

7.30 am 'Wakey-Wakey! Time to get up!'

I'm not getting up for at least half an hour.
I just want to stay here in bed.
And finish my dream about chocolate ice cream,
So I'm not going to hear what she said.

7.45 am 'Come on, lazybones!'

I'm not getting up for at least fifteen minutes—
I don't care a bit if I'm late.
I've already got three detentions. So what?
I'm still not getting up before eight.

7.58 am 'For the last time …!'

I'm not getting up for another two minutes—
Mum says I'm in trouble. She would.
But I'm not going to school where I'll feel like a fool,
Cos its's football and I'm just no good.

7.59 am and 50 seconds

I'm not getting up for another ten seconds.
I'm not getting up for another nine seconds.
… eight

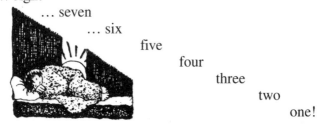

    … seven
       … six
          five
            four
              three
                two
                  one!

I'm not getting up. NOT AT ALL!

Laura Hughes

The Poet's Home Videos·

Floods

My favourite Spring days are days of dirty downpours
when the rain is so heavy that our brook swells
like a bruise until the banks are burst.
I am almost bursting as I look out the window
and I long for the rain to stall and stop falling.
Then I swear to Mam as I wear my wellies
that I won't take my little brother anywhere
near the swirling, whirling, wicked waters,
but they draw us to them as iron filings to a magnet,
or spaceships sucked towards a black hole.
We wander, meandering, two sticks in the flow.
He reminds me of Mam's words and that it's all my fault
if she finds out that we wade in the waters,
our wellies shlucking in the muddy currents,
playing games of splashing stones, building
dams of one hundred metres thickness,
four hundred metres high,
floating branches from wind-lashed trees,
wet in our wellies to over our knees.
Suddenly,
he falls and is in over his head,
perfectly safe
but completely soaked.
To the skin.
To the bone.

I drag him to the muddy banking, thinking
quickly all the time that we must get him dry,
or face the loud music of a mother's row.
So I force the stubborn child to undress
and hang his sodden clothes on a tree to dry
in the watery-weak rays of April shower sunshine,
as he shivers nakedly, only wrapped in my coat.
Of course it doesn't work and he's damp going home
and he smells as bad as a rotten compost heap.
I get the blame as I'm oldest and I'm grounded
                              in my room.

Staring out of the window, I notice that
a dirty downpour has begun again.

I can't wait for Summer.

Huw James

From Coming from the Bay

And so it is time to say goodbye . . .

                              Fresh-frozen

from the deep

               we come

puce-lipped and battered

                      bounding

over the bladed bladderwreck

                          to shiver and shake, to die

of cold—cry out

under the towel's coarse carborundum

We squeeze our bathers dry, shake out
the cold Saharas from our socks as
the whole Bay changes back,
shifting in slow procession up the stones . . .

                    After the last shoe laced
                    sandal strapped and towel rolled
                    our father lags behind
                    to scour the sand—religiously,
                    for any ring or coin or key
                    night and the tide might swallow

                    No. Nothing: nothing
                    but our stampeded prints—
                    hoof over hoof
                    cold, indecipherable

                    Alan Perry

Inland

This ship-in-a-bottle: his final gift to me.
It stands always on the shelf in the bay-window.

On rainswept nights like these, I look through glass
At the wild darkness outside; I put on some Sibelius,

Perhaps, and feel the room begin its slow unmooring.
I have lived in hills inland, alone, too long.

A swell glowers in the woodwind. Listen:
The tame fields outside turn to green ocean.

Beyond the bay-window, in the swaying evening,
Clouds furl like sails; the music lurches, breaking

Chords as white as frayed waves. The windsong
Is salt music that catches on the tongue.

Later, at dead of night, I sit in the window bay;
Hold in my lap his final gift to me;

Watch the darkness move; turn on the radio,
And hear the rhythms he moved to long ago:

Finisterre, Sole, Fastnet, Lundy, Irish Sea ...

Michael Ponsford

Fighting the Tide

On holidays, after seven and a half months
of counting the days since Christmas
(Easter is good—but there's only
so much fun in chocolate eggs),
After the excited sing-song journey
and me being sick, 'Every twenty miles!'
according to my dad,
we would go to the beach every day of the fortnight
and eat sandy sandwiches,
packets of family size crisps—each,
swig coke,
stuff 99s,
and each a whole chicken, or ham,
or at the end of the fortnight, a tin of spam,
between us.
The rest ate whole tomatoes,
(but not me, I don't like them—
'Fussy eater', my nan says).
But my favourite part of every day was
fighting the tide.

My sister, my brother and I would build
huge walls of sand,
defences against the battery of the tide's attack.
The design would change every time with
each of us arguing whether a pointed end would
stay standing longer than a rounded wall.
There was no time to decorate these sea walls
with castellations or crenellations,
towers or gates.

The onslaught of the tide was there to be fought.
We lost.
Every day.
But every day
we fought
just the same.

In the evening we would sit in the bar with the adults
fighting the tide of sleep.

At the end of the fortnight, I would fight the tide of
leaving.

Part of me is always with my brother and sister,
fighting the tide.

Huw James

43

From 'Letter from a Far Country'

(The saucers of marmalade
are set when the amber wrinkles
like the sea if you blow it.)

Jams and jellies of blackberry,
crabapple, strawberry, plum,
greengage and loganberry.
You can see the fruit pressing
their little faces against the glass;
tiny onions imprisoned
in their preservative juices.

Familiar days are stored whole
in bottles. There's a wet morning
orchard in the dandelion wine;
a white spring distilled
in elderflower's clarity;
and a loving, late, sunburning
day of October in syrups
of rose hip and the beautiful
black sloes that stained the gin to rose.

It is easy to make of love
these ceremonials. As priests
we fold cloth, break bread, share wine,
hope there's enough to go round.

Gillian Clarke

Blackberrying

Clutching lunch-boxes but not working,
we're off to the Waun
clambering over the stile
wellied and lumbering
between summer and autumn:
sun warming skin, wind stiffening bones.

Hopping the frog-pastures
we hear the donkey's raucous brays
making our giggles small as sparrows
and see in the distance
a shine of horses: white and brown
and fawn and mottled.

'Where are we going?'
'Down past Moody's field.'
The sparse brambles tangled
round fences have been picked clean,
the Sheep's Bit wags
its blue-brushed head in all directions.

Wild mint, hiding in the reeds:
inhale its smell to keep us going;
footballers on the Moody's
dodge the cowpat defenders;
derelict house behind leafy walls
spotted with cream flower-pods.

Searching the juiciest and biggest,
tips of fingers pricked by reaching,
stumbling on broken blocks and plaster,
filling our boxes with stained chatter:
tasting in one the sugar and sour
the grit and slither of the afternoon.

Mike Jenkins

.In the Garden and Back Lane.

In Gardens in the Rhondda

In gardens in the Rhondda
The daffodils dance and shine
When tired men trudge homeward
From factory and mine.

The daffodils dance in gardens
Behind the grim brown row
Built among the slagheaps
In a hurry long ago.

They dance as though in passion
To shame and to indict
The brutes who built so basely
In the long Victorian night.

Idris Davies

A load of coal

(in memory of my grandfather, killed in the mines, and in
tribute to the miners on strike, 1984-5)

A storm of hail
used to come to the gable end,
regular too, in season—
rough lumps of it
bright and clean.

The overseer there was Gran,
counting in more than a load
of 'compo' coal,
remembering that fireless morning
when the news came—
       an accident
below ground
       and Grandad in it.

The fire of life's so fierce,
so cold its embers—
the invisible scorch to the heart.

To us, grief means cheap coal.

After everyone else had left
she went to her solitary Aberfan,
to the shed, to fondle and reproach
hard coal that's never quenched.

Menna Elfyn, translated from the Welsh by Tony Conran

Nature

Spring
First week in dune, mourning due.
Phlox of sheep, there yous and lams
That haply gambled and barred.
The cheaping of birds, the sent of flours,

Spring whether in the hedge rose.
Routes that tern in the war
Mirth put fourth knew chutes,
Wight be loss am. The ere was wholly.

Summer
Son shone at hi noon, at lo tied
On the beech. Sum navel reck lay
In a creak from passed daze,
And serf broke on the sure.

Small buoys with spayeds played
Buy the see and built damns.
Turns swooped on muscles.
Inland, the waiving corn.

Autumn
Wry, maze and beens were in,
Buries hung in the lain and a well-healed
Girl road her hoarse upright.
Sun shone on September hays.

A prints was court and find,
Forbearing where he should knot bee.
The golden heir crumbled. No reign yet
In the blew hills of wails.

Winter
Moor friezing thyme. Bear trees
Weighted and there twigs broke at knight.
Eye sickles hung from Eve's and
Four too weaks no burred sang.

It was sew coaled, sew coaled.
The soil was pact like hard steal.
Owe that this to two sullied earth.
We red Frost to each other.

J. P. Ward

51

The Rain

I hear leaves drinking rain;
I hear rich leaves on top
Giving the poor beneath
Drop after drop;
'Tis a sweet noise to hear
These green leaves drinking near.

And when the Sun comes out,
After this rain shall stop
A wondrous light will fill
Each dark, round drop;
I hope the Sun shines bright;
'Twill be a lovely sight.

W. H. Davies

Pied Beauty

Glory be to God for dappled things—
　　For skies of couple-colour as a brinded cow;
　　　　For rose-moles all in stipple upon trout that swim;
Fresh-firecoal chestnut falls; finches' wings;
　　Landscape plotted and pieced—fold, fallow, and plough;
　　　　And all trades, their gear and tackle and trim.

All things counter, original, spare, strange;
　　Whatever is fickle, freckled (who knows how?)
　　　　With swift, slow; sweet, sour; adazzle, dim;
He fathers-forth whose beauty is past change:
　　Praise him.

Gerard Manley Hopkins

Snow

In the silence of snow
redwings are whispering
in firethorn.

An apple's orange skin
uncurls; birds peck
a flesh of crystals.

Kate Johnson

Psalm for 20th Century

Blessed are the hills that the acid rain kills.

Blessed are the trees dying of disease.

Blessed is the flower sucked of its power.

Blessed is the grass destroyed by the gas.

Blessed is the soil that we stupidly spoil.

Blessed are the clouds, the chemical shrouds.

Blessed are the rivers now they are sewers.

Blessed is the sand like mess in my hand.

Blessed is the sea that is oiled and filthy.

Blessed is the sky where the sick winds fly.

Blessed are the hens in their 'holocaust' dens.

Blessed is the grain grown only for gain.

Blessed is the fruit that we daily pollute.

Blessed is the meat that we cannot eat.

Blessed is the bird that is no longer heard.

Blessed is the seal that the knives unpeel.

Blessed is the air that our lungs cannot bear.

Blessed is the town that we bulldoze down.

Blessed is the child that the city drives wild.

Blessed is man and his 'live-for-now' plan.

Blessed is the Earth as we plunder its worth.

Peter Thabit Jones

Sunpoem

```
              o
             hot
              orange
             round
the sun is    old
             yellow
              atomic
             holl w
```

Peter Finch

In the Poet's Menagerie

Feeding the Bat

At first it was a small cold palmful
a hunched and sorry scrap, clenched still
but for an infinitesimal buzz and tremble

as we passed it from hand to hand
half fearful that the buzzing might explode
into uncontrollable flight. So we found

a box, and a place by the stove, and scrounged
a spoonful of dogfood from the corner shop
and waited. When the scratching started

we crowded round to listen: it was alive!
Lifting it out, it seemed larger; it moved
its clever head from side to side, gave

delicate soundings. Two eyes, dark points of light
gleamed, not at all blind, and long questioning
fingers gripped mine. Whiskered like a cat

with a cat's silken cunning it consented
to be fed from the end of a stick, opened
a triangle mouth wide, and dipped and lunged

manoeuvering meatlumps in. Laughing, we squeezed
waterdrops onto its nose, to hear it sneeze
minute bat-sneezes, to watch the supple greedy

slip of a tongue flick the droplets down.
As it warmed, it got bolder, nipping our skin
with needle teeth, unfolding its tucked wings

turning its goblin face to the window, where
milky chilled spring daylight lured
it to sudden flight, skimming at head height

a strange slow flutter, followed by a whisper
of displaced air. Awaiting a change of weather
we hung it in a bag to sleep over the stairs

and roused it for feeding. After the second day
it arched its back to be stroked, and played
a biting game, neck stretched impossibly

backwards, slyly grinning. That evening, the sun
shone. We carried it in its bag to a vacant barn
by the river. It squealed as I left it there, long

angry squeals; but I was firm. I would not
be quite a witch yet, stroking and feeding a bat
my ears turned to its music, swooping, flitting about—

though I lean out to the buoyant dusk, for all that.

Hilary Llewellyn-Williams

I hate flies

really hate 'em
loathe their filthy, disease carrying habits

tasting our food with their feet
vomiting
then sucking the vomit back up
with some of our food
mixed in
I kill 'em whenever I can

sprays, supplements, rolled up newspapers,
paperback latest sci-fi thriller
but a hand-towel is best
and for distance track-suit
bottoms held by the ankles

and now you say
they pollinate more flowers than bees do
THWACK!!

That's something I'll have to
think about.

Labi Siffre

Truth's a Dog

Truth's a dog that snarls and drips saliva on
your carpet.
It's also one that licks your hand and sleeps in
front of the open fire.
Truth's a dog that growls one minute—
and whimpers the next.
Truth's a dog on a lead.
But then the lead snaps and the dog runs away.
Truth's a dog that guards and protects.
Until one day it finally turns against you.
Truth's a dog that is always coming or going—
and then one day it is gone for good.

Melanie Wagstaffe

Old Cat

For Gwenno, who's at least 21

Another winter dawn. I can't remember
how many mornings we've begun together,
me sipping tea, she lapping top-of-the-milk,
crunching Munchies, licking her rusty silk.

Like an old woman with a shabby coat
she dabs an old stain with a bit of spit,
combs her knots out with a tongue-washed paw,
then sits half-dreaming at the Rayburn door.

Old cat! Her walk is heavy now, and slow,
her coat is rough: One winter day I know
there may be no one at the morning window,
only her paw-marks across fallen snow.

That morning, I'll switch on the kitchen light
and she won't leap to the sill out of the night,
her green eyes gleaming, silently mouthing 'O!
Let me in out of the wind and snow!'

But here she is again with a cry at the door.
I open it a crack to wind and sleet
and a handful of flakes. She delicately shakes each foot
and prints her daisy-chain across the floor.

Kettle and cat and stove will doze together,
adjusting old hearts to the icy weather.
All day the house will simmer with her purr,
like a loaf rising, the lift and fall of fur.

Gillian Clarke

Avocado

Let us now praise
my breakfast avocado:
under whose unpromising
dinosaur skin
the green flesh creeps
brightly.

Fiona Sampson

Three Jovial Welshmen

There were three jovial Welshmen,
As I have heard men say,
And they would go a-hunting
Upon St David's Day.

All day they hunted
And nothing could they find
But a ship a-sailing,
A-sailing with the wind.

One said it was a ship,
The other he said Nay.
The third said it was a house
With the chimney blown away.

And all the night they hunted
And nothing could they find
But the moon a-gliding,
A-gliding with the wind.

One said it was the moon,
The other he said Nay.
The third said it was a cheese
And half of it cut away.

And all the day they hunted
And nothing could they find
But a hedgehog in a bramble bush,
And that they left behind.

The first said it was a hedgehog,
The second he said Nay.
The third said it was a pincushion
And the pins stuck in wrong way.

And all the night they hunted
And nothing could they find
But a hare in a turnip field,
And that they left behind.

The first said it was a hare,
The second he said Nay.
The third said it was a calf
And the cow had run away.

And all the day they hunted
And nothing could they find
But an owl in a holly tree,
And that they left behind.

One said it was an owl,
The other he said Nay.
The third said 'twas an old man
And his beard was growing grey.

Anonymous

The Last Tiger

Soon there will be no more of us;
I am the last of all my tribe.
Here I wait Oh my father and mother
My fangs rotted to stumps and black blood
Amongst the clapboard hovels of the suburbs.
Here I wait Oh my sons who never were,
In the days of my dying,
The gun shot festering in my hollow side,
Filling my belly on the wind.
Here I wait Oh my ancestors
Amongst the tin cans and the dustbins
Gnawing at my broken paw,
The mighty kingdom of my spirit
Shrunk to a white hot tip of hate.
Here I wait Oh my cousins
To kill this old woman
Who will limp across the cinders
With two buckets in her hands.

But I have a dream Oh my gods,
I have a dream
That in my ancient burning strength
I will roam the cities of mankind
And screaming claw the stolen coats
Of you my honoured sisters and my brothers
From the backs of rich and beauteous ladies;
Thus, do not ask me why I hate women.

Gareth Owen

Red Spiders

Red spiders, just hatched,
running across sun-warmth of a wall
over lichen like bits of red lichen

in all directions at once
as if they'd spilled from a scalding pot
and couldn't stop till they cooled.

A microscope would zoom up
their humourless eyes, the mouth,
eight legs' relentless traction over the pitted

terror-surface of the stone,
while the eye bent over the lens
reflects on the relevance of scale.

John Barnie

The Hare

A solitary hare
On an immense cliff-side
With his ears pricked
& his long
Furred feet
Ready to scuttle.

& I put the fear of god
Into him,
Clapping my hands
Like a devil in the air,
& he bolted home.

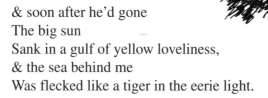

& soon after he'd gone
The big sun
Sank in a gulf of yellow loveliness,
& the sea behind me
Was flecked like a tiger in the eerie light.

& I looked about me
With my ears pricked towards the silences,
& when the great, mysterious sensibility of night
Clapped its darkness high above me,
I didn't dare linger,
I bolted home too.

Dylan Jones

.In the Poet's Laboratory.

Miss Third World

(from the Welsh of Hywel Gwynfryn)

The girls are all assembled—
Go to it, darlings, go!
Are the judges at their tables?
Then on, boys, with the show.
It's just too bad—let trumpets play!—
Miss Ethiopia's kept away.

They've got the lot, these lovelies,
Their glitter cuts a dash—
They bought it all in Oxford Street
For who-cares-how-much cash …
But have they, in their boudoirs curled,
An ear for the groans of Miss Third World?

There's white wine, red wine, salmon—
Tonight we're in Cockaigne
With trough on trough of caviar
Swilled down with pink champagne …
And Miss Third World, hey, what's your lot?
'Two children, dead—that's what I've got.'

'I'd like to visit Hollywood
And hobnob with the stars …'
'I'd like to ride in Voyager
And take a look at Mars …'
What, Miss Third World, is your delight?
'To make it through another night.'

Miss U.S.A.'s a stunner,
Miss Spain's a lithe gazelle,
Miss Germany's voluptuous,
Miss France is t*rès, très belle*.
But one, alas, is less endowed—
Miss Ethiopia in her shroud.

The queen of queens is chosen!
How winsome she appears,
Outpouring as per usual
Brief crocodilish tears.
But when, Miss Ethiopia, when
Will your wet cheeks be dry again?

Nigel Jenkins

What's the time?

What's the time?

At the first strike
The time sponsored by Accurist will be
Time to wash the grass
Before the sheep can eat it
And it gets around the class

What's the time?

At the second strike
The time sponsored by Accurist will be
Time to hose the sky
That cool dome of blue
Where peace doves used to fly

What's the time?

At the third strike
From Accurist
It will be time to give the clouds a sweep
The dust gets in the eyes
And makes the whole world weep

What's the time?

At the fourth strike
From Accurist
Rainbows are fading out
The ends are dripping into streams
And poisoning the trout

What's the time?

At the fifth strike
From Accurist
It will be time to wash the rain
You wash it and you wash it
And you rinse it down again
And you wash it and you wash it
You can't be really sure they say
Until you've rinsed it and rinsed it
And you've rinsed the wash away

What's the time?

I've asked the time
From Accurist
And this is what he said
'I can't tell you what the time is
I've suddenly gone dead.'

Betty Lane

They held up a stone

They held up a stone
I said, 'Stone,'
Smiling they said, 'Stone.'

They showed me a tree.
I said, 'Tree.'
Smiling they said, 'Tree.'

They shed a man's blood.
I said, 'Blood.'
Smiling they said, 'Paint.'

They shed a man's blood.
I said, 'Blood.'
Smiling they said, 'Paint.'

Dannie Abse

Ballad

If we launch the boat and sail away
Who will rock the cradle? Who will stay?
If women wander over the sea
Who'll be home when you come in for tea?

If we go hunting along with the men
Who will light the fires and bake bread then?
Who'll catch the nightmares and ride them away
If we put to sea and we sail away?

Will the men grow tender and the children strong?
Who will teach the Mamiaith and sing them songs?
If we adventure more than a day
Who will do the loving while we're away?

Gillian Clarke

Gadgets

'Gadgets gets you into trouble,'
I heard an old man say,
As he plucked a stone from a horse's hoof
While the beast tried to look away.

'They gets you into trouble,
As I know to my cost;
It's alright relying on gadgets
'Til one of them gets lost.

I had a little gadget
That could plant seeds in the spring,
But I lost it in December
So I couldn't plant a thing.

My garden came and went that year
With nothing growing in it,
No runner beans, no hollyhocks,
No fun, you should have seen it!

Another little gadget
Was a present from my brother
But I never found a use for it
For some reason or another;

I kept it in my pocket
Waiting for a chance to use it
'Til a mate of mine came to borrow it
And what did he do but lose it?

Gadgets cause you all kinds of pain
And I tell you it's no joke
To have a little job to do
With a gadget that's got broke.

There's a gadget for cutting nostril hairs
And another for buttering spam,
But my favourite is a twisty thing
For scraping mould off jam.'

Phillip Jackson

So Far

apples are computers
beaches are creches
cars are loud-hailers
days are entitlement
earth is afternoons
fuel is decorum
grass is chrome yellow
hills are athletics
industry is sculpture
jeans are photography
kinship is unlikely
law is new physics
murder is abandon
neon is moonlight
offices are funtime
people are exceptions
quiet is recalled
rivers are fibreglass
sky is orchestral
tarmac is helium
understanding is microdot
victims are neighbours
water is consumption
x is all over
youth is authority
zeal is the extent

Peter Finch

In the Poet's Album.

The Poetry Magician, My Mum

She's the director, the head, the boss,
Although her toast is burnt
And baked beans lumpy
As mushy swamp water.
She sits in her favourite chair,
And holds you with the glittering
Blue eyes of the Ancient Mariner.
Peering through the gold rings of intelligence,
Balanced on a small snub nose
Above two pink lips,
Which took us to different worlds,
From that old pink sofa.
I was there when the Highwayman
Met his grizzly end,
When the Ancient Mariner
Was telling his story,
When Laura went to the Goblin Market
And the Lady of Shalott's
Magic mirror finally cracked.
This character in patchwork coat
Red shoes and long coloured scarf,
Would entwine me in all these stories.
She who doted over her old films
And *film noir* books.
She gave me the confidence
To walk the high wire.

Zoe Brigley

There's a Face

Oh there's a face!
Where you get that hair from?
Got it from a old tom cat.
Give it back then, love.
Oh there's a perm!

Where you get that nose from, Lily?
Got it from my father, silly.
You've got it on upside down!
Oh there's a conk!

Look at your complexion!
Oh no, *you* look.
Needs a bit of make-up.
Needs a veil.
Oh there's glamour!

Where you get that smile, Lil?
Never you mind, girl.
Nobody loves you.
That's what *you* think.

Who is it loves you?
Shan't tell.
Come on, Lily.
Cross your heart then?
Cross my heart.

Dylan Thomas
from *Under Milk Wood*

Steps

The first step was visiting.
He brought flowers.
They would dine,
Play music, laugh late.
Then, one morning,
He was still there.

The big step was the marriage.
A pagan bridesmaid,
I romped anxiously,
Threw confetti, pricked
My fingers on her roses,
Wished my dad was there.

Living together, I was
Always out of step,
The unequal angle
In a two-sided triangle.
On walks she gave her hand
To me, but gave her mind to him.

At night time now,
Upon the stairs,
I shut my eyes and shrink.
When little, I scaled
This mountain range and
She redeemed my night.

Gillian Fothergill

In Memoriam
—to a sailor

In a strange, unclamorous host, the dead
And the seaweed tangle;
Pearl parlours, acres of fish
Are tomb to learning's splendour.

R. Williams Parry
(translated from the Welsh by Tony Conran)

Snap. Shots.

the first time i saw
my mum take her teeth out
i thought it was wonderful
must have been five
and i tried and i tried
but i couldn't get my teeth
to slipping' and slide out
no way could i capture
the click an' no doubt
as she took her teeth out
the matter o' fact
as she clacked 'er teeth back

it's unfair
that i have to wear
his old trunks
un-sleek
unlike any others on this beach
mum-made of maroon
coloured wool waterlogged
heavy with blackpool
couldn't swim if i could
inadequate dignity
one paddle backing
slack elasticity

twenty feet up
unassailable
never go back
and they'll never know where
anyway they don't care about me
so i'm staying forever so there
right here in this tree
that'll teach 'em a lesson
for mistreating me
i wonder
if Mum's made a cake
for tea

over the hills and far away
to once upon a faerie tale
of fabulous friends in fun pretendings
ever after
happy endings

Labi Siffre

Local boy in the photograph

There's no mistake I smell that smell
It's that time of year again I can taste the air
Clocks go back railway track
Something blocks the line again
And the train runs late for the first time
Pebble beach, we're underneath a pier just been painted
                                                    red
Where I heard the news for the first time
And all the friends lay down the flowers
Sit on the bank and drink for hours talk of the way they
                                                    saw him last
Local boy in the photograph—Today
He'll always be 23 yet the train runs on and on
past the place they found his clothing.

Stereophonics

Epitaph for Uncle Johnnie

Here lies a tenor. For his grace rejoice.
His soaring notes rang out, the rafters rang.
He gave God glory with his golden voice
And lived the silver music that he sang.

John Ormond

Bedwas Boys

Bedwas Boys know all the tricks
Bedwas Boys are tough, like bricks.

Bedwas Boys are built for speed,
Bedwas Boys don't follow, they lead.

Bedwas Boys know how it's done,
Bedwas Boys chew rocks for fun.

When Bedwas boys go out at night,
The fiercest dogs forget to bite.

'Cos Bedwas Boys have flashing eyes,
Muscles like iron and teeth like pearls.

And the only thing they're scared of
Is those terrible Bedwas Girls!

Phillip Jackson

In the Poet's Playroom.

My Friend

My friend
he laughed
and laughed
until
he turned
into
a rub-
ber ball;

he bounced
and laughed
and laughed
and bounced
out of
the bath-
room down
the stair
through open
doors to
here and
there;

down the
path and
out the gate
we miss
him now
too late
too late!

too late
to tell
him that
we care
too late
to lend
too late
to share.

although
we see
hin bounc-
ing by
we don't
say much
too shy
too shy!

Phillip Jackson

A Letter

I took a letter to the post
and then I lost it.
How could I have? It was
in my pocket.

Perhaps somebody stole my letter?
When they open it
they will see it's to you
from me.

My letter won't mean anything
to them. The story
I had to tell you's private.
It goes:

I took a letter to the post
and then I lost it.
How could I have? It was
in my pocket.

Perhaps somebody stole my letter?
When they open it
they will see it's to you
from me.

My letter won't mean anything
to them. The story
I had to tell you's private.
It goes:

Fiona Sampson

Bells of Rhymney

O what can you give me?
Say the sad bells of Rhymney.

Is there hope for the future?
Cry the brown bells of Merthyr.

Who made the mineowner?
Say the black bells of Rhondda.

And who robbed the miner?
Cry the grim bells of Blaina.

They will plunder willy-nilly,
Say the bells of Caerphilly.

They have fangs, they have teeth!
Shout the loud bells of Neath.

To the south, things are sullen,
Say the pink bells of Brecon.

Even God is uneasy,
Say the moist bells of Swansea.

Put the vandals in court!
Cry the bells of Newport.

All would be well if—if—if—
Say the green bells of Cardiff.

Why so worried, sisters, why?
Sing the silver bells of Wye.

Idris Davies

Dreams of Flying

Over trees
with the breeze
I float
I gloat
As I rise
Wind sighs
I move
Land dies.
Little cars
Little bricks
Little roads
Little sticks
and the people little dots
in their cars little spots.

I sink in the air
And rise without care.
On my wings
Movement sings
As I hover in a dare.
And beneath my feet
Tiny bricks in the street.

And I almost collide
With the birds in my ride.
And the clouds all rush by
as I dash through the sky.

Like a cloth that is spread
On a fine feathered bed
The fields are laid
Like a table that's made.

And I feel like a king
And a great awesome thing
I grow near to the sun
And my journey is done
But my wings melt away
I am fading away
and I fall from the sky
as birds echo my cry
And the world spins around

As I'm nearing the ground
grinding and winding
and the ominous sound
of whooshing air is there
like standing alone
at the top of the stair
and losing the ground
til with a whoop through the head
I land in my bed
and wake up with a start
and pant in the dark.

Jude Brigley

Rock'n Roll Poem

be
bop
a
ropity
bop bop
a
bop bop
she rop bop
a
rama lama
ding
doop
doo waa
a
dum dum
dum dum
dummy
doo waa
shad doya
doip doip
doya doip
bop bop
arooooo
shad a ra
ooooooo
waa waa
hey bop
a re bop
a she bop
a tee bop

a wee bop
rop bop
aloo bop
alam

bam
       boom

Peter Finch

Creepy Crawly Pie
(A Welsh witches' recipe)

Beetles, spiders, worms and bugs,
put them in a pot and stir in some slugs.
Ladybirds, ants, flies and bees,
mix them together and add a few fleas.
Pour on some slime, throw on cockroach spice,
whisk a pinch of salt and a thousand woodlice.
Blend a dozen eggs with milk that's sour,
and boil in a cauldron, for half an hour.

Darren Moody

Cool

Now some people think I'm too young to be hip
But if you think like that you'd better button your lip.
For child of the eighties, I move with the time.
And not only that but I can tell you in rhyme.
If you want to be hip and get into the groove
You've gotta know what to wear, you've gotta know how
                                                    to move.
Get rid of that gear it clutters your head
You've gotta slip into something that locates you instead.

CHORUS
If you wanna be hip and get into the groove
You've gotta know what to wear, you've gotta know how
                                                    to move.
You've gotta be cool, cool, cool.
You've gotta be cool, cool, cool,
You've gotta be coooool.

Try Reebok, Nike, Benetton, Levi-strauss
Or Snoopy, the Simpsons, Pink Panther, Mickey Mouse.
Ease on a jacket that's been lying on your bed
Put Adidas on your feet and ruffle up your head.
Try some shades for your eyes and a cap worn askew
You never chose your clothes they just grew on you.
Now put this all together and try to act cool
'Cos dressed like this baby you'll be nobody's fool.

Poetry Unlimited

The Poet's Hall of Heroes.

The Women of Fishguard

The Emperor Napoleon
He sent his ships of war
With spreading sails to conquer Wales
And land on Fishguard shore.
But Jemima she was waiting
With her broomstick in her hand,
And all the other women too,
To guard their native land.
For the Russians and the Prussians
He did not give a damn
But he took on more than he bargained for
When he tried it on with Mam.

Their cloaks were good red flannel.
Their hats were black and tall,
They looked just like brave soldiers
And were braver than them all.
The Frenchmen took one look at them
And in panic they did flee,
Cried ooo-la-la, and then ta-ta,
And jumped into the sea,
And said to one another
As back to France they swam,
We'd have stayed at home if we'd only known
That we'd have to take on Mam.

The Emperor Napoleon
He was a man of note,
His hat was sideways on his head,
His hand inside his coat.
When he heard the news from Fishguard
His sorrow was complete,
Oh Josephine, what can it mean?
My soldiers all are beat!
I'll make my proclamation,
Though a conqueror I am,
You can conquer all creation
But you'll never conquer Mam!

Harri Webb

Rebecca and her Daughters

There's a stirring in the hedgerows,
There's a clink of bridle chains,
There's a gathering in the by-ways,
There are hoofbeats in the lanes,
There's a secret army rising
To set the law to right,
Rebecca and her daughters,
Are riding through the night.
  Riding, riding,
  Riding through the night.

For the tollgates are a burden
On the poor folk of the land,
And the word's gone out in whispers
They shall no longer stand.
There's a people out of patience,
They would rather strike than wait,
Rebecca and her daughters
Are riding to the gate.
  Riding, riding,
  Riding to the gate.

With torches and with axes
She has cleared the country roads,
Proclaiming that the highways
Are free for all men's loads,
And as she smashed the tollgates
On the path to liberty
With Rebecca and her daughters
We'll ride to victory.
  We're riding, riding,
  Riding till Wales is free.

Harri Webb

Excalibur

I am carrying his sword,
arm's-length through the dark wood.
In the rear, two armies dead,
Arthur dying.

Glittering, finest in the world,
on its hilt two serpents coiled,
precious stones in beaten gold.
Throw away the sword.

At half-light, reach the lake,
hear the small waves break
and the wind in the reeds.
No, I saw nothing.

Get back, find him coughing blood
(not one dram of what was spilled),
knights gone to the sandy ground,
women to convents.

He will find out, and rage.
Do what the rule-book says,
look towards a later age.
They will glorify him.

Keep before their eyes the gold,
the song, the glamour of the blade,
and dry bones stick through Arthur's shroud.
Throw away the sword.

All dead, I alone
to keep the legend riding on.
And the sword winks in the white sun.
Throw it.

Merryn Williams

103

Grendel's Mother

They are feasting in their halls,
mead, harpsong, lights at the doors
as I creep over
the drenched sand, pools standing seal-grey.
Pain has gnawed me all day.
They will sleep soon. Sure-footed,
I approach them.

Yesterday they killed my son,
Grendel, man-monster.
Above the hearth men nailed his arm
and traced the black clots of his blood
to the lip of the water.
He lies now on the channel-bed.
Beowulf slew him.

Off guard, they will not sense
me drawing nearer.
Inland, up the pebble ridge
through the sea-lavender
and across that long-barrow,
men raised above their fisher-huts,
to some dead hero.

In the small hours, I
will cross their threshold,
rush them, maul men where they lie
and leave lumps of flesh scattered—
too small a price for my son!
Before the spring tide is down
I will kill them.

Tomorrow that young man
will plunge, radiant with anger
for his dead friends, with clean sword
through the dark water
and claim me, the last victim.
The troll-line will be lost. My blood
will melt his weapon.

Merryn Williams

My Land

She is a rich and rare land;
Oh, she's a fresh and fair land!
She is a dear and rare land—
This native land of mine.

No men than hers are braver—
Her women's hearts ne'er waver;
I'd freely die to save her,
And think my lot divine.

She's not a dull or cold land:
No! she's a warm and bold land;
Oh, she's a true and old land—
This native land of mine.

Could beauty ever guard her,
And virtue still reward her,
No foe would cross her border—
No friend within it pine.

Oh, she's a fresh and fair land!
Oh, she's a true and rare land!
Yes, she's a rare and fair land—
This native land of mine.

Thomas Davis

·The Poet's Pitch·

Footballers' Birthdays

Matthew was born on Monday,
A winger full of pace.
Thomas was born on Tuesday,
A striker who keeps his place.
William was born on Wednesday,
A defender full of charm.
Tim was born on Thursday,
A goalie who did no harm.
Franco was born on Friday,
A player whose crosses were deep.
Samuel was born on Saturday,
A full-back whose place would keep.
And the mid-fielder born on Sunday,
Would score for us all.

Barry Webster

Death of an old Footballer

He was ready when the whistle blew
Laced up both his boots
Jumped up smiling from the bench
One of life's substitutes.

Raised his arm to the popular end
Flexed the suspect knee
And out of habit showed his studs
To the eternal referee.

Gareth Owen

Netball

I'll field at silly mid-off,
In the nets I'll gladly bowl.
I'll hit a googly for six.
I'll make a wicket fall.

> *Chorus*
> But don't ask me please.
> I'll repeat it so you'll know.
> Don't ask me—to play netball.
> Not   netball.
> Not   netball.
> Don't want to hop on one leg.
> Don't want to stretch out tall.
> Don't want to turn on one foot.
> I don't like netball.

I'll try to be a goalie,
I'll dribble past the team.
I'll kick the ball into the net
So crowds will cheer and scream.

I'll bully off with gusto,
I'll sprint the length of the pitch.
I'll tackle when the ref's not looking
And score without a hitch.

I'll even go into the pack,
In the muddy scrum I'll shine.
I'll give a long pass to the wing,
Get it back and cross the line.

I fancy playing tennis,
Love-40 and receiving serve.
I'll return the ace with a winner.
I'll be the Sampras of nerve.

Jude Brigley

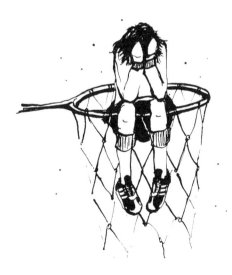

Rap: Street Hockey Queen

I'm the Street Hockey Queen
I'm fast and I'm mean
I look great in my Bauers
And I practise for hours
I'm the rollerskate queen.
When I give 'em a roastin'
Boys say that I'm boastin'
And it can't be a joke
Watchin' my wheels for smoke
And I'm nothin' but trouble
When I'm burstin' their bubble
'Cos I shake at the double
I'm the Street Hockey Queen.
I'm the dude in the mood
I can play pretty good
With a stick in my hand
I'm no babe in the wood
I'm a street skating beauty
But I'm nobody's cutie
I am fast and I'm mean
I'm the rollerskate queen.
Consider my prowess
Remember my name
I'm beatin' you boys
It's no longer your game.
I'm headin' for triumph
Oh aint it a shame
There's a dame with her name
In the Street Hall Of Fame.

If I was a guy, then you'd think
I was cool
'Cos I got the talent
To make you all drool
I got the nerve and the verve
Just like one of your own
But I'm usin' my brain
'Stead of testosterone.
I'm fast and I'm mean
I'm the Street Hockey Queen,
YEAH.

Brian Smith

One of the Chosen

The jerseys are already down, marking the goals.
We've tossed for who's United,
And who has to be City.
Now we're lining up you can see who is
Confident of early selection.
The duffers and the duck-eggs shuffle
And push each other,
Pretending they don't care about being
Last when we're up the bus-terminus field
Picking sides for footy.

Speedy and Gaz are the captains,
Always.
'I'll have Woodsy,' says Gaz, choosing the
Nippiest winger on our estate.
And grinning, Woodsy goes to stand behind
His best mate.
(Once, Gaz chose Rat Rogers to be a goalpost,
And Rat stood there, a human upright, dead proud
That Gaz had noticed him . . . just glad to be
Included.)

Speedy points at Dekker Brown, a sporting centre-half
Who thumps you if you go
Round him.
'Tommo'
'Ken'
'Des'
'Slogger'
The talented, the powerful and those with class,
Already pencilled in,
Their names put down at
Birth.
'We'll have Smiffy,' says Gaz.
At last.
(And after all it is my ball.)
I leave one line to join another,
Breathing easier now I'm one of
The chosen.

Brian Smith

147

It's the magic number: seven more
than black despair, and that last black
has to be the hardest. He poises
his cue, and we all feel sick

with certainty: he won't make it.
That black is every job interview
we failed; every final step
we tripped on. It's every no

we heard when we needed to hear yes,
and it's going to happen again,
it's bound to … There's the contact: too late now,
it's paused on the lip; we all breathe in,

and it's down, and everyone's going mad,
because destiny's taken a day off
and we've won. His laughter radiates
out at the audience; they mirror love

back to him, and everyone wants
to hold him, touch him, touch the luck,
in case it's catching. He did it
for all of us; he put down the black.

Sheenagh Pugh

Leisure

What is this life if, full of care,
We have no time to stand and stare.

No time to stand beneath the boughs
And stare as long as sheep or cows.

No time to see, when woods we pass,
Where squirrels hide their nuts in grass.

No time to see, in broad daylight,
Streams full of stars like skies at night.

No time to turn at Beauty's glance,
And watch her feet, how they can dance.

No time to wait till her mouth can
Enrich that smile her eyes began.

A poor life this if, full of care,
We have no time to stand and stare.

W. H. Davies

Traveller

Where are you going to, walking, walking?
And what is in your pack?

I'm travelling to an unknown land
With my years upon my back.

And what do you hope to find there?
And will you find a bed?

I'll find me a bank of sweet dark earth
And pull it over my head.

Gareth Owen

And so goodbye and don't forget to visit.
The poet's house has doors which open wide,
And many more rooms you could discover:
You won't know how or where until you've tried!

ACKNOWLEDGEMENTS

The editor and publishers gratefully acknowledge the generosity of all the poets and also the co-operation and permission of the publishing houses and trustees listed below:

Seren Books for the work of Peter Finch, Catherine Fisher, Mike Jenkins, Kate Johnson, Christopher Meredith, Robert Minhinnick, John Ormond and Sheenagh Pugh;

Carcanet Press Ltd for the poems by Gillian Clarke;

The trustees of Mrs H. M. Davies Will Trust for the poems by W. H. Davies;

Meic Stephens for the poems by Harri Webb.

'They held up a stone' by Dannie Abse first appeared in *White Coat, Purple Coat* (Hutchinson);

'Feeding the Bat' by Hilary Llewellyn-Williams first appeared in *Poetry Wales* magazine;

'The Last Tiger', 'Death of an old Footballer' and 'Traveller' by Gareth Owen © Gareth Owen 1995 are reproduced by permission of the author c/o Rogers, Coleridge & White Ltd, London;

'In Memoriam' by R. Williams Parry appears in the original Welsh version in *Cerddi R. Williams Parry* gol. Alan Llwyd (Gwasg Gee 1998);

'Grendel's Mother' and 'Excalibur' by Merryn Williams first appeared in *The Sun's Yellow Eye* (National Poetry Foundation, 1997);

Lyrics from 'Local Boy in the Photograph' (Jones/Jones/Cable) © 1996 are reproduced by kind permission of Universal Music Publ. Ltd.

'There's a Face' is an extract from *Under Milk Wood* by Dylan Thomas (Dent).